I0838741

SCARS

an anthology of microlit

edited by

Cassandra Atherton

SPINELESS WONDERS
www.shortaustralianstories.com.au

Spineless Wonders
PO Box 220
STRAWBERRY HILLS
New South Wales, Australia, 2012
shortaustralianstories.com.au

First published by Spineless Wonders 2020
Text copyright © remains with individual authors.
Cover image and design by Bettina Kaiser

Editorial assistance by Linda Bathish.
Layout by Bronwyn Mehan.

Typeset in Franklin Gothic Book
Printed and bound by Ingram Spark
ISBN 978-1-925052-48-0

Scars, an anthology of microlit/
Atherton, Cassandra (ed)

Distribution in Australia and New Zealand by New South

A catalogue record for this book is available from the National Library of Australia

I don't have tattoos, I have scars!
Marina Abramović

Contents

Preface

An anthology of scars is a recitation of being. Not because it must be. It (un)simply is. This collection is for anyone who has ever lived. At all. Of any moment. In any time.

It is perhaps tempting to tend towards the epigrammatic. Scarring and its examination can be the stuff of inspiring frames, aimed to propel an over-coming. These pieces do not offer pithy truths or an abbreviated clutch of motivation. Instead they dwell, haunt or jostle with the nerves, and act in many ways like affective palimpsests that are variously variegated, nuanced and syncretic.

The scope of entries considers scars from an extraordinarily diverse range and scale – the permutations of Country, landscape and region; the exquisite immensity of the granular; and the sediments and inflections of interstitial topographies of sense. Some are subtle renderings, all shadows and scintilla. Some hope to jar and scratch. Still others are unapologetic in their welt.

The thematic arrangement these works provide include sets of oppositions: transplant and uprooting; concealment and exposure; ancient and modern; traversals and stasis. At other times, there are contrasts and uncomfortable enactments: sites and sights; sacred and bone; flesh and palette; words and incisions; forms and pre-texts.

This is just to name a few. Cassandra Atherton has been

delicate in her editorial arrangement, and publisher Bronwyn Mehan has created an exciting platform for microlit in this beautiful publication. Their exceptional skills further enrich already fertile registers.

Scars: An Anthology of Microliterature is a complex, liberating and painful sensorium. A relatable, accessible and well-inhabited site created with exquisite craft by all its contributors.

Breathe. Hold. Enter.

Gabrielle Lorraine Fletcher 2020

Samuel Wagan Watson

HERE THERE BE MONSTERS

*['Here there be monsters...' refers to
Cartographers' remarks once placed on
old nautical maps to warn seafarers
of possible peril in rogue and uncharted
waters.]*

Billy Mooks' mirror told him he was a prune. The blackfulla steeped in a swell of self-loathing. Rips and burr wrinkled features; a pestilence ravaged topographic map of country. His tribal blood-soil, sold for a ticket to the Big Smoke. The last of his people reduced to his last cent, having gambled it to dust.

He stared and stared. Mirror-mirror on the wall, who's the most narcissistic blackfulla of them all?

Tarnished fingertips explored accordion cheeks, flashes of his father's eyes in the film of his own, a slight refraction of light focusing into mirrored distortion. A crevasse of skin in his right-side jowl pulsated open. Black claws, darker than his own, ripped his reflection in two. Billy Mooks' eyes bulged as they witnessed the stealing of his final breath; confession of the thief stolen in the wake...

Siobhan Hodge

HONG KONG RESIDENT

I don't tell my mother where I am headed. The lift shakes as I reach the ground. Typhoon nearing shore, but only a black rainstorm warning so far. Each step down the hillside threatens spillage. I have to pick lines in islands of pavement, slip taxi taillights to cross. I don't tell my mother that I can see them. Students in black, clotted on Harcourt Road. Teargas mists between forests of arms, legs, mouths. Theirs is the cry. I hover in air-conditioning, hair in wet ropes. Offer smiles as they sit in the cool, hands on phones, hearts on lips. They rise like water, roar in waves that chisel rock. I slip past the riot shields lingering in the park. Permanent resident, a cracked spine. Toe the steps back up the hill. I tell my mother about the sales, how the posters were torn down. No queues in the MTR. Yellow post-it notes peel like scales down my eyes. Home is a passage, disappearing under the current. I don't tell my mother where I am headed.

Judith Nangala Crispin

ON FINDING CHARLOTTE
IN THE ANTHROPOLOGICAL
RECORD

We meet on the surface of a photograph, as a fish and bird might meet in a lake, at some point of sky and the water's plane. Charlotte, in a book called *The Aborigines of Northern Victoria*, sits jade-black on earth, wind disarranging her hair. Trees obscured by falls of campfire ash. Her nudity is covered by a blanket. I don't know if her breasts are hanging, if her thighs bear designs or marks. A needlework of scars crosses her chest, repeated dots, like patterns on a goanna's back, like rain spat by goannas into dirt. Soon constellations will appear over branches, on this night of ninety years ago, this never-again night – and she asks me: "Where did you go girl, with your made-up history, your ever whiter babies?" This is what remains, a record of relatedness – scars to hold the memory of someone precious after they've died. We begin by cutting skin – rub wounds with gum and ash, black ants to cauterise the flesh. I remember them saying: don't worry, this blackness fades with each generation. Charlotte is a map of Country stained by massacres: Skull Creek, Poison Well, Black Gin's Leap. A geography of skin and land – maps for the returning, for those who speak only a murderer's tongue, whose songlines are erased, who consulted departments of births, deaths and marriages, who stood beside rented Toyotas, clutching photographs, in a hundred remote communities, asking strangers "Do you know my family? Can you tell me who I am?" This moment, an old light is crossing the boundaries of emulsion, and I say to her – Charlotte, Grandmother of my Grandfather, I am Judith, and these are my scars.

Benjamin Laird

REPEAT, AFTER ME

→ [1]...[11],
→ [1][11]↺,
→ [11]...[1],
→ [2][4][6][8][10], or
→ [1][3][5][7][9][11]

[1] in each pattern an ending, a pause in sequence, to begin [2] i rewrite myself like a smooth path cut through long grass [3] attempting to resist succumbing to the obsessions invisible but for ritual [4] to practice an atheism in prayer and devotion to saint dymphna [5] a religion, constructed with mathematics, that processes the machinery of control [6] in which programming embeds error and i call myself in recursion [7] the skin splits reflecting a riverbed in summer, burnt from exorcism [8] the fragile walls strain while the crow caws at the windowsill [9] that this is the spirit escaping the pressure of complete collapse [10] today will start like it was tomorrow and will be yesterday [11] and recognise that every pattern without an ending is a prison

KA Rees

NO WHITE M&MS

How the colour from m&ms stains your fingers before you get to the centre, how a game of cricket lasts five days and no one dies of exposure, how the heads of jonquils dance even as their necks are breaking, how children's laughter spreads like wildfire but our hair fades to ash. My white skin pits like the shrivelled seed of a peach, the moisture long since gone from the flesh. How black men and boys were chained together on Rottnest Island, how you can go there and camp and there are quokkas and you can Instagram it. How absence itself is a memorial but amnesia is a national past time, how buildings tower into the sky like solidly built things, but how a brick fits solidly into a hand, how bricks once came from sand. How there are no white m&ms only ones sucked of any colour.

Andrew Roff

LANDSCRAPE

We stand back from the puckered lip, wary of triggering a collapse. The top of the cut is graded and degraded, scrubbed of scrub, and nothing holds anything else together. From up here it's impossible not to feel the weight of the absent rock, and our task seems impossible. Umber churned to gravel-grey, the surface not denuded so much as stripped.

No one could hope to heal. Our task is remediation, a different thing. When the syndicate quit the site, hauling salvage up the rails, shrugging its corporate shoulders at the pursuing mob, and chanting 'Insolvency!' like an appeal to Saint Benedict, the work fell to those who had loved this place before, when saplings and worthless soil hid the coal seam.

We will mend as best we can. Marred, marked, what is returned will be unfruitful, nothing more than a biding. At the end of the world, the creek beds baked, plastic vomited up on all the beaches, the birds unable to rise but still calling questions, this ground will split. Ghosts will remember what was done.

Gabrielle Lorraine Fletcher

CARAPACE

Sometimes I am on my Country.

'I am one of you,' I tell my Spirit Ancestors, 'but I struggle with chromatic aberration and feel neutered all the time.'

Out of dapple, within rustle I hear their affirmation: 'You are you, and us and all,' they say. 'Your bleached skin a scar that keeps and tells our Truth.'

I am still and they repeat 'Keep moving.'

I take this as a sign of work to do, so speak in circles to commandeer the scrimmage of straight lines. My obligation is to burr the lens of other knowing.

Shady Cosgrove

MAGIC SHOW

She was the magician. Her ex-husband, the beautiful assistant. He gathered props and posed at the side of the stage, smiling with those straight, white teeth. After she impressed the crowd with interlocking hoops, he climbed into a long box with his head and feet at either end. She held up a blade and sawed through his torso, wheeling him around. When it was time to piece him together, she waved her cape and disappeared to smoke and murmurs. People stood. The ex-husband's face was pale, blood pooling on the floor. He let out a small groan and finally someone, in the wings, called for an ambulance.

Paul Collis

SCAR MAKERS MAKE MEN

You can never see how legend has been told to young fullas.
You could never see how we shake and were scared.
We initiates, whisper questions to quiet our shaking, to Biamai.
No longer under the protection of mother,
But on solid ground, our Mother Earth, we stood. Ready to be
cut, in the shadow of our history.
Law re-told by senior men strengthened our backs – we boys
stand together, solid.
And we stand alone.
This is the way we become men.

Skinny legs trembled;
Biamia, speak Barkindji to me.
Yaparra yaamari. Yaarmari.
Murranta. Murranta

The tremble and worrying in us is broken at the sound of his
voice.
We stand strong, in law,
now as men.
We take our place in history.
Knowing now, how we are important.

Paul Collis

UNTITLED

They cut us when we went through law – they cut our body, and they cut the tie from our childhood, and cut the tie from our Mothers.

We become Keepers of tradition and law

We became men, scarred.

Raelee Lancaster

BACKSEATS LIKE BATHROOM STALLS

Slow like lines to the bathroom—like lines in the bathroom. We sit in your car in a haze of smoke and chatter: shatter half-dreamt dreams before our bad decisions disrupt them for us. My brain moves too fast and words get glued like peanut butter to the roof of my mouth. You sit in anticipation, hanging onto my every word as if you don't already know what I'm about to say. We're in-sync that way. You know the shape of memories I buried more than a decade ago.

Night leaks darker through the window, the half-wound glass stuck like shards in a broken wing. Words turn liquorice in red-peppered mouths. We use the moon as a safety net and spill secrets onto your backseat; burn ash and broken thoughts into the leather. You cover the stains with your jacket and tell me not to worry, we'll clean it in the morning.

You promise that next weekend, we'll do this again. Sober, this time. But this routine has become our Sunday solace. When we return: your jacket, those stains, bathroom lines—they'll all still be here.

Anna Forsyth

DRAWING THE LINE

I like to capture their essence. To see the real person, but it's all about the line, ya know? I didn't, but I nodded. *Can you pass me the charcoal?* I peeked nervously around the easel at the woman, all soft peach-tinted flesh perched on the stool holding her sleeping baby in her arms. Her long, dark hair was flecked with grey. Jared was measuring angles with a pencil. Squint; measure; repeat. *It's all in the details, Tab.* This time I rolled my eyes. It was half-way through the lesson that I realised I'd hardly drawn more than a line. How long had I been staring? With the baby now in the other room, I could see everything. Every undulance. I swallowed, wondering why it was so unnerving. I steadied my hand to follow the line of the scar as faithfully as I could. I glanced at Jarred's drawing. He had sweat pooling under the arms of his plaid shirt. *Jared. Where's the scar?* He paused just for a moment. *Oh, I didn't like the line, so I left it off.* I stared at him, touched my belly gingerly. *Somehow, I don't like the line either.*

Paul Hetherington

RIPPLE

Beneath the white shirt a ripple of tattoos, and damage from trapeze acts when you fell, after swinging out into space like a sudden verb. The gap between past and future closed; your muscles propelled you into netless air, and mainly you stayed aloft, like a word among emptiness, or rapid, undecidable metaphor—spangling light, a gust in the Big Top, a clenched expression in glittering dark. Cast limbs and torso, a swivelling turn and hold. White light on your body falling like a shirt.

Stuart Barnes

OLD HABITS DIE HARD

with a line from William Shakespeare's A Midsummer Night's Dream

Every weekday afternoon, until my father collapsed, my mother and I would laze in their recliners and scoop homemade French onion dip with Jatz Crackers. The way she'd move the nailfile from digit to digit without tilting her gaze from *The Young and the Restless* was mesmerising; so, too, the hopeful glint of the grooved stainless steel. *Did Mrs Cashion hide it in a fruit cake?* I'd sometimes wonder. My father the crazy quilter still picks his fingernails until blood floods the lunulae; his nail beds are cratered as the moon's. I've been biting mine since middle school; not even the solution my mother would apply to the unholy mess could stop me; I grew to enjoy its bitterness as I grew to enjoy grapefruit's. Psychiatrists insist trichotillomania goes hand in hand with onychophagia, but recently I met my eyebrowless ex who otherwise resembles Johnny Marr and who's only ever clipped his fingernails. 'I tweeze them,' he said. 'The Zoloft's useless.' I started plucking my left one after the accident. 'You look like Aquaman,' Kane said, prodding my bald patch as we exited the cinema. The course of true love never did run smooth. Thank God I'm able.

Steve Kinnane

TWO SKULLS

I prepared a bed of paper bark and gum leaves for you, separate from my sleeping sons.

I didn't tell my boys of your visit. I left with you in the cold, dark of dawn, quietly smoking the house with Balga resin before our journey, keeping you with me.

The airport X-Ray revealed your tragic beauty; two skulls, an adult and child, perfectly clean lit luminous green. I held your tiny cardboard coffin more firmly, protectively. My fellow travellers.

Broome welcomed us with a warm breeze filled with the scent of pindan, mangroves and salt. As we drove, I talked. I described the rangelands, the Kite Hawks circling, the communities we passed – windows open, dry heat, dust and the sounds of the bush.

I avoided everyone, passed crops of hitch-hikers – straight to Fitzroy Crossing.

The Cultural Bosses were waiting. Without fuss they lit the tin drum filled with Brearley and gum leaves. Together we were smoked good and proper – cleansed by the thick, liquid grey smoke of our Country. And then I let you go, gently, as you joined so many others who are gathered here, waiting.

Tomorrow, the Rangers are coming to carry you home to Country.

Jessica Wilkinson

SCORES

1. Words cut across the court *fat, awful pants*. (Outer thigh in E flat)
2. They're giggling, I'm meant to hear. (Inner ear for chamber choir)
3. From a great height, splits and a high-pitched howl. (Forehead in G major)
4. She's gone, we bury her in the rain. (Left ventricle, trumpet solo)
5. Mother says: "Why are you doing this to me?" (Full-throated silence [lumpily])
6. All those eyes sharpened at my bones and my skin. (Armpit in C for violin and cello)
7. He's lying. It is obvious. (Stomach, just the high hat, uncut version)
8. I'm lying. I sink into the dirt. (Left index finger for electronics and vibraphone)
9. He draws up charts and spreadsheets; I unspool a trip-wire. (Left index finger for jazz quartet)
10. One visible mark, at the knee, round and smooth. (A single semibreve, held by a lonesome oboe)

Nadine Schofield

SHOT THROUGH

The couple walk up the path in the dark. They have forgotten the head torch, but they know the way and there is some light from the moon. They stay right. Left of the path are the remnants of the old railway line; wooden pillars like broken teeth shot through with rusted bolts and grass.

On the other side of the path, and beyond the wire fence, is the working line used by the mine. They had been caught in the myopic headlight of a diesel train on the way down the mountain, the driver held the horn and the woman held the sides of her head in discomfort. When the train had passed, she turned to her husband.

'Another one.'

He had seen it too; the red penis graffitied on the last carriage. There were penises spray painted all over the village, on every road sign and brick wall.

Now, as they pass the village monument; a lump of coal suspended in a rusted circle, they see the dead doe. She is hard up against the fence and stiff in the grass. The black orb eyes are milky in the moonlight and the woman cannot look away.

Jude Bridge

IN YOUR FACE

Sick of being invisible? Had a fancy haircut and no-one noticed? Why not consider designer scarring? Here at We Scar U, we use traditional methods to create truly unique face art.

For that "bad boy" look, one of our fully trained consultants will punch you artistically in the face with a knuckleduster. Our staff are skilled brawlers who can accurately work a fist from cheek to cheek or forehead to lip, depending on your preference. Jagged edges for authenticity can be added at no extra cost. You'll be amazed at how quickly you'll attract new friends, eager to hear about your scar. Imagine telling them about your foray into cagefighting, or how the police roughed you up in what was clearly a case of mistaken identity!

You don't have to go large, we cater to all. A simple slash from a razor blade will neatly divide your eyebrow in half with minimum pain and recovery time. Tell your eager new friends how you could have lost an eye if the parachute hadn't opened!

Each scar comes with a lifetime guarantee. If it fades or disappears, we'll replace it free of charge.

We Scar U
The cut you deserve

Colleen Russell

A TOMATO FOR ALICE

Alice had buried three husbands, all involved in WWII. Jack was never the same after the battlefields of Europe. Good men gone, their faces now fading.

She was content to live alone. She went to bed when she wanted, ate what she liked. Her interests kept her busy. People overwhelmed her; she pushed them away.

Her neighbour was a foreigner of some sort. Alice was obliged to be pleasant, but deliberately ignored him.

She nurtured several rose bushes in her small yard, and a herb garden, fresh for the table. A choko vine draped the back fence, but she had to beat the local kids to the fruit.

Alice's yard was her own battlefield, fighting snails. At dusk she collected them in a bucket of salt, and that got 'em! Peering through the fence one evening was the rugged visage of Mr Whatshisname, smiling, nodding agreeably. He must think the snails are for my dinner. How hilarious! She grinned, couldn't help it.

'Is hard living on pension, no? Me, also,' he said. 'I have many vegetables; we share, yes?' and he gave her a tomato.

Alice laughed– and gave him a rose.

Aedan Siebert

BANANA STRING

I ate a hair once. Swallowed it down with a hunk of manchego.
Well almost. Jenny was pissing herself. I was dying. I can still
feel it sometimes, thrashing around my larynx like a worm. Not
sure whose it was. That's the worst bit. Stranger danger by way
of follicular DNA. These days Jenny waits until I'm mid-chew. Not
like I need the reminder. Jenny reckons it's a phobia. All I know
is that I steer clear of banana string

Oliver Mestitz

TROUBLE AT THE MEN'S SHED

His middle name was Trouble. That's what someone had told him a long time ago, before he'd lost the ability to distinguish between the faces that existed in memory and the faces constructed by dreams. He had a scar over his windpipe, two bisecting lines in a sagging X. He had a name for each line: Benson and Hedges.

Someone must have given him a Christmas cake. It was a Lions Club Christmas cake. It was encrusted with mould that smelled like blue cheese when pierced with a butter knife. We all told him to throw the cake away but choosing to ignore us was one of his few remaining pleasures and we had no right to deny it.

He removed the mould from the Christmas cake like the skin from a cantaloupe and sculpted the remaining clumps of flour and sugar and rotting fruit into cubes to store in the freezer. It was a tiny freezer, full of pork chops. I've eaten worse things in the war, he said, trying to make room in the freezer. We all groaned. He turned towards us, his neck and shoulders clenched. It looked as if the scar was smiling.

Julie Chevalier

BADGE

I asked if she had any experience I could include in her resume.

Any Certificates? Diplomas? Jobs?

No eye contact but she took her fingers from the cross on her necklace long enough to hand me her overseas driver's licence. A blurred photo. Black head covering, eyes with dark circles.

What kind of work are you looking for?

My English is bad.

In an interview you could say, 'I am studying to improve my English'.

Each time I saw her at the Centre she looked younger, more like a uni student. The third meeting I handed her the resume.

Now catch the bus to Dress for Success to get an interview outfit. No animal prints, fake jewels, logos, cleavage.

I not wear sleeveless.

Good. You want something covered up, plain. I pointed to my own slacks, shirt, shoes.

No one see bullet holes.

Ten months after starting the meatpacking job, she reappeared at the Centre.

Boss of assembly line now! You add to resume, please?

She draped a denim jacket over a chair, patted a tattoo of a pistol on her puckered left bicep, extended a ten dollar bill.

I want give back, please. Top up new asylum seeker's Opal card.

Dan Disney

SYNTAX ERA

>>>

and without notice or consultation, the shift epistemological, our screens surrounding us wholly now and *The Game* our only coalition, immersive Thing, real as feelings once were felt (now banned), real as neon darknesses in which we each parlay our unsleep

>>>

ever since electric eyes first peered from binary gloop, our avatars (tilt-necked, mouths indistinguishably pinched) had sounded alarums of such little consequence that we'd barely hear the interpellations, of course our daze pre-packaged, droll, a feature in the design

>>>

in *The Game* we are kith snaking through immersions of random probability, expressing data into spatial patches and no-one asking ever 'do my desires look big in this oculus,' amid the neurally-networked convolutions and the sex-bots where money buys nought, we're ripple effect, a static skein through social places, no more than artificial breeze (comptrollers moderating, **'do not say** *Game,* **reticulants, this is your creed and narrative'**) at our DeepDreaming screens, underneath all quivering monstrosities (**update pixels, propagate forward, find gradient, propagate downward**) neither fear nor pain but a numbly orphaned ecstasy compelling us, dreamers, onwards and deeper toward the multitudinous blasts of lonely orgasm

Jan Dean

FEAR, OR FLAUNT

Scar, villain of *The Lion King*, exemplifies 'by name and nature' through his deep slash from forehead to cheek. Was he of good character and therefore unblemished before the fight that endowed his moniker? A scar suggests an abyss, like an iceberg with ninety percent below surface; a cavern of hatred, seething away. Masks are often scarier than the scars they cover. Much depends on your viewpoint. One woman's scab is the beauty spot of another. Famous charmers like Gloria Swanson and Elizabeth Taylor were naturally endowed with birthmarks, but history also points to artificial ones, patches in the form of moons, stars and hearts for syphilis sores or smallpox scars, from the sixteenth to eighteenth-century in France. These *mouches* or 'flies' resembled insects alighted on skin. Not all cultures hide blemishes; the Japanese concept of *wabi-sabi* considers 'impermanent' and 'imperfect', highly desirable qualities. In Japanese aesthetics *kintsuki* is the use of precious metals to repair broken pottery, so the piece is more attractive and greatly valued. During his search for the elusive indigo dye, iconic designer/craftsman William Morris wore permanent blue stains up to his elbows: Beauty born through discolouration or unwanted marks. Smiles trump tears.

Trisha Pender

SHARK BITE

The **shark bite** is what my partner calls the scar where my right breast used to be. Cup size H would you believe. I wonder what they did with it.

Given its size, I thought I'd at least lose some weight when they removed it, but the hospital food was so bad I put it all back on in a week. Either that, or the bathroom scales were dodgy.

My mother took me bra shopping to a specialist boutique, purposefully named *You Really Are Beautiful!*

The fake boob you put in your mastectomy bra is called a **form**. A form for swimming is made from silicone and resembles a large **jelly fish**.

The best temporary forms are made from memory foam **(mammary foam)**. But there's a special delight in receiving a pair of hand-knitted knockers from your McGrath Breast Care Nurse TM. Why a pair?

If you need to weight them down a bit, you can try a) **sinkers** b) **sandbags**.

Josh (Mei-Ling) Dubrau

ATAPS 2013: (THE DEPARTMENT OF HEALTH ACCESS TO ALLIED PSYCHOLOGICAL SERVICES SUICIDE PREVENTION PROGRAM)

At the parent/carers' night you leave your suicidal kids at home. The room creaks; a thickening critical mass of uvulas, glottal swells of dark-rimmed Mums who say, "I haven't slept in weeks."
Their dams are at the break-point.

I sleep, TKO'd by meds myself. Since the time I muddled up the symptoms of the flu and an OD, I'm sloppy with the lockbox concept too.
Who am I, to stop, to set, *anything* in order, motion, or in stone?

I always find fresh razor blades. Such hate towards a small waxed envelope seems strange. Cuts I only catch when long sleeves slip from shoulders. The mask is quickly straightened.
A pick-up run on laundry day/week/month retrieves a bandage left in no-mans-land.
Its browning roughness bears no trace of any blood I've ever seen on TV or in 'real life'. If that's what this is. I rub the crepe into my cheek, like my drawn blood could make hers disappear.

They question us as well.

Our own behaviour; is it simple?

Is it still self-harm if it was just your boyfriend's name you cut into your fourteen-year-old calf?

My mum puts up her hand and asks if biting fingernails badly counts.

Megan McGrath

BABE

The truck shudders as Faye pulls up on the gravel shoulder. As soon as the air-con conks out, the central Queensland heat fingers its way into the cabin. She reckons she's got about thirty minutes until she's gone too far to turn back.

She gets out. Wind rushes through dry grass as a road-train roars past. She checks her phone. No call-backs.

In the tray, the full boxes taunt her. The heat makes her scar itch. She rubs it below the waistband of her jeans. The gravel puffs a dust cloud as she scuffs the ground, thinking.

Her passenger rolls down the window, juts a flanno-clad elbow on the frame. 'Babe?'

'Just give us a sec.'

He is not at all like her Gary. He calls her *babe* and grabs her arse. He drinks her in like she is a cool stream to his endless thirst.

Technically, she hasn't done anything wrong yet. She could boot him out, drive home, forget all about it. But the promise of something thrilling, dangerous, unexpected, tugs in her gut.

She's left lasagne for Gary in the refrigerator. Milk for the baby. Her phone illuminates in her hand, silent, incoming call from *Home*.

Tereza Crvenkovic

PINK LIFE

We were joined together stitch-by-stitch, under the glare of star-like surgical lights. I was her saviour, a perfect kidney, delivered from a desperate mother to her death-branded daughter.

The girl was everything to me: my world, my star, my universe. I worked blood hard for her while she birthed her dreams. Together, we swam through seas, embraced love, created magic.

After two decades, I slowed; I strained to push through the murk. Nightmares where she was sentenced to die haunted her. Soon we learned I was dying.

If they could speak, her scars might tell you of all the near-deaths we fought during this time. Yet they'd remain mute, her softest parts silenced, sewn over, sealed deep inside. Secret pleas for life and – at times – death.

Now I'm a tiny flicker. But I know when I'm gone, my shape, where I remain inside her, memories of our life together, will continue, until she's gone.

And her? She lies again on this table, pale, older, illuminated on the threshold of a new life.

Here comes my replacement! Pink, shiny, full of pulsating possibility. The masked, sky-blue people lurch towards her.

She's prepped. Open. Ready to receive the hope of new life.

John Blackhawk

DOG LIP

we always thought you had a hare lip...

Bounce the ball up high - head it back up into the air - catch.
Bounce the ball up high - head it back up into the air - catch.
Bounce the ball up high - head it back up into the air - catch.
Bounce the ball up high - head it...

Thought I'd been shot. Fell sideways onto the sand with forty five kilos of dog on top. Blood spattered on my shirt as I got to my feet. Pressed a finger to my lip and it parted like curtains. It went through to the gum, blood dripped off my elbow. Distracted from his seagull chase by this new game he needed to join – he'd sprinted, launched, and smacked my face with that rock of a skull.

In the surgery getting stitched the doc found it funny - *You'll be scarred for life. It'll be a memento of your dog. He's left an impression on you!* He left me in stitches but not in a good way.

Returned home to an oblivious dog, lying on the carpet scratching his ear - *Where you been dad ? It's late. Where's my dinner?*

Richard Holt

THE SHEAVES OF DAYS

Sam O'Lachlan's blade catches the interminable sun. The thinning redgum no longer shades the dust. The creek that has sustained it through all the O'Lachlan generations hasn't run for a year. Growing feed is no longer important — there's nothing left to keep alive. The few cattle Sam couldn't sell are on agistments far away. Those too weakened to be relocated he shot and buried. The river to the north is nothing but pools, hardly fit for mosquitos. The birds have flown. And, with summer bearing down, there's a hint of smoke haze on the breeze. Even with nothing left to protect, there's no peace in this country.

Sam takes the knife and draws a line next to the others, one to mark each day since the last rainfall. Ninety-four now, in clusters of five, the way prisoners record their incarceration. The bunches, each bound by the horizontal slash of the fifth day's mark, suggest cut hay gathered as it was in the early days, when droughts could be easily forgotten during the good times. Sheaves of days circle the trunk. A glance at the sky says Sam will be back tomorrow to complete another bundle.

Chris Cody

MILLION-DOLLAR QUESTION

Dick was climbing out of the car when his neighbour called down, 'I got worms in my gutters!'

Dick looked up. 'What's that?'

'Worms!' The neighbour said. He took a handful of something black and held it out. 'Can you believe it?'

Dick laughed. 'No,' he said. He leaned back into the car for the bottle of champagne and heard a dull, wet thud.

'How 'bout now?'

Dick pulled out and saw the dark clump of soil on the roof of his car. 'Jesus, Burt.'

'Told you!'

Inside the clump squirmed a dirty pink worm.

'Didn't I tell you?'

'Well what's it doing up there?'

'Ahh!' cried Burt. 'Now that's the million-dollar question!'

Dick watched the worm trying to dig down into the roof, then swept it onto the lawn. 'I'm going in,' he said.

Burt called, 'You figure it out, come tell me!'

Dick went in.

Sandy was at the kitchen table marking papers. 'He's been up there all day,' she said. 'He's lost without Mim.'

Dick was laughing. 'He just threw a worm at my car!'

'A worm?'

'A worm.'

'Like a worm worm?'

Dick held out the bottle, then got on one knee. 'Like a goddamn worm!'

Deb Wain

DISCUSSING PAIN [AND THE THINGS I DON'T SAY.]

No, not an injury; I was born with it. [Kintsugi – rupture made visible, the damage and its repair.] A spinal malformation of the vertebrae, L4 or L5, I can't remember which. Better since the surgery; before, I couldn't walk without excruciating …[No adequate words for pain. It escapes our language and our memories.] I used to drive around looking for a close parking space, now I'm running again. Hadn't been able to run or ride since I was a teenager. Definitely worth it. Ten hours on the operating table – in through the back first, then the front, then back again. Three operations in one. Yes, a bargain, three for the price … [I was afraid I might die.] About twelve months to fully recover, three months before I could drive. Not quite pain free now but it's manageable. Some impressive scars, yes. [Intimate lines: navel to pubic bone, lumbar to sacral.] Like the bionic woman… [Metallic angles, structures that will outlast impermanent and imperfect bones.] …yes. [Kintsugi uses gold or silver; mine is titanium.]

Rosanna Licari

MARE TRANQUILLITATIS, 1969

It was a smooth landing on the rocky satellite that dominates the night sky. The Moon's complexities became apparent long after we discarded myths and magic, and we declared it a mix of Earth and a heavenly body. Our half-sister. The scarred child of a savage collision that magnetised the Earth, granted it a new tilt and spin, producing the diversity of cycles: the seasons, day and night. The Moon pulled tides over fledging biospheres and kindled our taste for hypotheses. Our eyes locked onto black and white TVs as Armstrong declared *Houston, Tranquility Base here. The eagle has landed*. And the Moon took a deep breath.

Magdalena Ball

EARTH SCARS

An object of darkness travelling fifteen miles a second came into close collision course trajectory. Lost in the glow of the sun. I thought of the earth, receiving the blow in her solar plexis. Uluru-Kata Tjuta, Northern Territory. Radiating nerves and ganglia.

What it would look like? Two million hectares of rivers, forests, floodplains exploded instantly into impact winter, such terrible alchemy. The crisscross of lines across distended hips, tears concentrated to amber.

Is it easier if it's random? If there was nothing we could have done? I could be there, first in the queue, taking the hit for our planet, sensing motion as the rock enters the atmosphere, a new species in deadly motion, riding the shockwave of exogenesis.

There are other scars, below the crust, keloids of overexpression; of industry – we're an industrious race, always working, growing, metabolizing, metastasising.

Proof runs along the fault line in warning shades of phosphorous green. Tailings   digging   burning   tunnelling   cutting   liquid reserves in aqua blue, iridescent blooms and red tides, the trace of radionuclides, carbon spheres changing the signal in sedimentary rock layer, arriving faster than the speed of sound, crashing before the sonic boom of impact.

Dominique Hecq

DARK ENERGY

A thwack. You sink into yourself. An explosion of elementary particles. You are a supernova shooting through air and stars. A baryonic ball of bleeding energy scattering matter in the void. Your heart beats out of place like wind gusting on a high plain. Pulse hovers on a knife edge. You wriggle out of your body. Crawl through gaseous clouds to a rocky alcove they call emergency. Climb the lookout they call a chair. Fall into antigravity. Whizz through a constellation of voices eying your soul from the back of beyond. When you come to Nurse Adani tells you not to touch your stitches. Or it will scar. You take your eyes off her badge. Stare at her face as though through a telescope. This is what a black hole looks like in a spark chamber.

Patrick West

SHOTGUN

Shotgun shacks are not to be confused with riding shotgun. Shotguns for short, they take their name from the avenue of air created when all the doors are flung open. You can fire a shotgun through the front door and hit nothing bar the scarecrow standing out the back.

When people think of shotguns they think of the poor and desolate of America; they think of towns without magnificent avenues; but these ways of thinking are out of date. Examples are legion. Only the other day, the National Enquirer announced that a derelict shotgun was to be shipped to Singapore to provide a talking point in the foyer of the Shogun Hotel.

Still, that sort of thing, riding shotgun on history like that, can't help but leave a scar. Somewhere.

Kathleen Bleakley

SWELL

from your ankle to bum, bruising after the fall, no cut but bleeding
beneath skin, blues to purple, yellow - jaundice like, blackening,
swelling foot, hurting, looking at you, as much as the final wrench
of us leaving old friends & family, bushlands, kangaroos among
the burbs, lake, four seasons: cicadas constant, tossing amber
leaves to a cloudless sky, frost melting at lunchtime, cherry &
plum blossom kisses.

our coast home: gazing out at the swell, you trying on shoes to
house this foot in transition, still blue below the surface, swollen,
as with flight, it will land again, plant on sand, feel grains between
toes. there'll be no scar.

Brenda Proudfoot

NEIGHBOURS

The man stands on his spade. The blade cuts deep into the clay soil. He digs in compost; turns and breaks up clods.

Two boys dart from behind the squat trunks of palm trees; machine-gun each other across no-man's-land. His seven-year-old son chases his playmate, grabs the waistband of his grey shorts, pulling him over. They tumble onto the grass.

The father looks up when he hears their belly laughter. His boy is fair; the other, dark with almond eyes. His mother appears from the brick house next door. She bows to the man. He nods, raises one hand to touch his brim. She reminds him of a porcelain doll: her delicate frame, her hands tucked into her sleeves.

'Osamu,' she calls.

The man plants seedlings in orderly rows. How long since he plotted the grids their Hudson flew over the Pacific, while hunting enemy ships? Since they killed his school mate, a Burma Railway slave? All that death and destruction ...

Now the Japs are living next door.

He washes his hands then stands back to admire his handiwork. Soon there'll be scarlet salvias and sunflowers drawn to the light.

Jen Craig

KITTEN

Last night, after a dream about a kitten—when I realised I didn't even think (in the dream) to look after it—that I wasn't even capable of looking after it—I knew there was something wrong in me—that something inside was caught up, stopped. And yet when (as I thought) have I ever looked after anything properly? When have I, at home, while passing a plant, whose roots are pressing out, swollen, through the holes at the bottom of its pot—pressing out so hard in its search through the silt for a crack in the concrete, the pot's on a tilt—when have I ever been able to pause in what I was doing to cut off the plastic shell, to change the soil, to trickle in water as they show us on Youtube? And what kind of person am I, I thought, who thinks she is kind—*who knows* what to do but cannot do it—this inner-stiff part of me—this scarred unyielding line that tugs my anemone limbs inside—prompting me to act or rather, *not* to act—holding me tight so that all out there might pass me by?

Alyson Miller

CONTRAILS

A faultline, kicking out from the bottom lip. No one can remember how, just another skin tear, though your mum has stories from bike-falls and chicken spots to the knuckle-print of that last backhander. In the botanical gardens, you stroke the trunks of trees shinned by possums and children, the bark grooves a broken song about gravity and rib cracks and flight. The landscape of your hometown is as guttural as my German great-aunt, and just as entombed in the wrong side of history, riddled with ditches and the echo wails of wild dogs pockmarking the mountainside. As a child you climbed rooftops to watch for smoke curls and plane glides against hot skies, your knees crazed with the kisses of brickwork and slate. Your father's chest is a geometry of lost things, a tessellation of moonshine and dead months and too many crosses to bear. You dreamed of alien hands reaching inside that heart-space, feeling against the corrugation of sinew and bone to pull out a crayon, a bottle cap, a legless doll. In the morning you burnt sheets and pillows in the cast iron pit, a snow-dust of ash and memory settling on the windows and lawn.

Susan McCreery

AFFINITY

You saw them first, from the hot glare of the cove. Cleaving the surface, they were, in gleam and dip. One leap and we knew. Between us one mask, one snorkel for air. I grabbed both when offered, and raced for the water, pulling myself out to the endless green where I thought they were, and they were. You, tiny, waiting. Then, in columns of light, it was just me and them. I dived and finned as they did. Sped up to spray-blast the sun, then down again. Each, when they passed, held my eye, seeming to grin. We drew closer. Must be old, that one, I thought, with its rubbery skin, crosshatched, marked. Still playing, though, still seeming to grin. It knew me, I thought, but most likely did not. No more than you. This ocean could carry me too, I thought, marked, grinning, out or in.

Danielle Baldock

BEST OF THREE

She waits. Watches yellow fingers of light slide across the airless room.

This one? He pokes a perfectly round scar on her tanned shin.

Well, I was five, in the supermarket...

Just the facts, Ma'am, Competition rules.

Spiky shelf, stabbed leg, Barbie reward.

Score! His eyes are alight.

This? She pokes a surreal white squiggle on his shoulder.

Skateboarding, 12, May's Hill. Blame my brother.

She snorts. So you say!

He grins. Next?

She holds out her foot, crisscrossed by a neat railway track, a crater midway down. Foot squashed by a rocker full of cousins, infection, operation, bonescraping, three weeks hospital, jelly oozing out.

Impressive!

She jigs in her chair. Beat that!

A jagged silence flows about them.

You know I can...

She bites her lip, leans to kiss his forehead.

The monitors beep fast, the lines showing the beats left in his heart swoop up and down.

He grips her hand, tries not to breathe too fast.

No way! She smoothes the bandages on his head. No-one can beat Oozing Jelly!

He smiles up at her then. Best of three?

And they sit close together, the clock ticking down, and go for Best of Three.

Christine Howe

THE 884ᵀᴴ

We've had this conversation before. Each time, you say there are some scars that will never fully heal. Ever. We've discussed this once a week, on average, for the last seventeen years – 884 times. It always ends the same way. You say it's impossible, I say it isn't, and we both finish up knowing we're right.

This time we're in bed, side-by-side under the woollen doona you say is not warm enough and I say is too hot. I'm about to say there is always potential for healing, but it seems glib.

I've seen deep cracks of pain in you before. Now, I see light, easing like lava through all those dark fissures. You're a kintsugi pot, broken pieces held together by gleaming seams of gold.

I prop myself up on my elbow so I'm looking directly into your face, the kink of your broken and re-broken nose. I don't say the thing I've said 883 times before. This is what I say:

'What if they become something *more*?'

You listen.

'I'll think about it,' you say.

I'm still waiting for the 885th conversation. It's been weeks now, since I stopped trying to convince you I was right.

Brenda Mattick

THE THIN WHITE LINE

If you happen to search for 'Iokea', Google helpfully assumes that you really want to wipe out an entire weekend by assembling bits of Swedish Flottebo, Fritids, or Flekke. I didn't.

So I broadened my search, typing 'Iokea village png'. And there it was, online – the source of my scar, a thin white line.

We were walking back along the hot grey sand after a fishing trip. The sharp tip of a knife used to gut fish pierced through the canvas fishing bag I was carrying. That neat cut on my leg became badly and dramatically infected, so next morning we walked along jungle tracks to a tiny medical outpost. The penicillin worked.

Not a big scar, barely noticeable now, this thin white line. But an offline link straight back to the village of Iokea in Papua New Guinea, to the warmth of my host family, massive sweet mangoes, acoustic guitar music, coconut husk toilet 'paper'. Scary ancestral spirits. Lilting Toaripi dialect. Roasted corn, yum.

My thin white line goes back in time. It was 1973 I was 19. And Google helpfully tells me that Ikea flat packs first came to Australia just two years later.

Shaynah Andrews

THE OCEAN HAS MADE PROMISES

Stockton; the girls painted watercolour *Lepidoptera* and gorged on their father's oranges and stuffed lumps of coal into their socks to keep them grounded. Boys loaded containers on the docks and held the black dust in their lungs and wielded rocks with their mates.

There is lichen on the headstone, now, of their sister/daughter/ friend. Bone-white sea shells and a pinwheel in a jar that has cracked apart in a storm. We light fires in old washing machine drums, howling at the orange orbs of super moons and blood wolf moons, before tipping the fluid from our menstrual cups into begonias and fiddle leaf figs to make them strong. We remember when the boys took us to their bedrooms and crushed our windpipes and called us bat-shit-crazy-whores if we weren't grateful.

One-eyed felines wrestle beside the ocean-rusted shipwreck on the break wall. Ladies bring them reusable shopping bags filled with Whiskas. They say the scars that weren't cat-fight inflicted came from fish hooks brandished by cruel kids. But the ocean has made promises. She gnaws away the beach, devours the old surf club. Then she breaches the great big houses, those glass nests, and shucks them of their young.

Carolyn Abbs

TRAGEDY

From the fourth floor, Canary Wharf, I watch office workers scurry alongside the murky docks. Lowry figures on film. I swoop down with my phone lens, swift as a gull. Workers wear sneakers for speed: fluorescent tangerine, shocking pink, lime green. Wires in their ears. Robots of a sort, muffled with scarves. They clutch coffees in colourful reusable cups: glass, plastic, ceramic, bamboo… I'm wondering if this is merely a fashion statement, when the theatre of my brain opens up like a stage: workers in kitchens washing their cups. Hot water gushes from taps, steaming up windows. Gingham tea towels flap to the chat of office gossip, the cost of a cup against the horror of polystyrene. My phone beeps. A friend shares a pic of landfill on the news last night (a screen within a screen): mountains of waste shipped, who knows where. I recall first year lit, how tragedy tightens like a screw. Words of fear appear on screen like a poem written to an image: *Watch out, it will return. Strangle us. Finish us. Full stop.*

Mark O'Flynn

THE PEACH TREE

The peach tree beyond the fly-strewn window took years to declare itself. Reason being the gouged trunk full of rot, spreading year by year, up the trunk and out the lateral branches, spilling sawdust like a punctured doll. Half the year it looked dead. How long have I looked at it before thinking this? I considered chopping the whole thing down, planting another, but each year as the rot spread, blossom erupted like a snow storm vivid in fistfuls of unthrown confetti. Some final blooming a few days a year before the winds laid waste and birds returned to feast, comparing last year's scarred harvest to this. I feel lucky with what chance has left, a few days flowering, the sudden profit of staying in one place a long time. The more puny the fruit the more blessed the flower.

Anna Kerdijk Nicholson

THICKER SKINNED

Strange, I've not written about you before, as strange as not seeing you by my mouth in the mirror. Yet you were remarkable to others. Like the comic 'you could be a ventriloquist's dummy if you had one on the other side', the lacerating 'hey girl, did you cut yourself shaving' and the incisive (from a French chirurgeon) 'you really should have sued'. I volunteered for you when I was nine, when I had a vain inkling, and here you are fifty years later, faded as my hair, crestfallen as my jowls and nestled into them in your usual 'make yourself at home' way. The comics, lacerators and surgeons don't seem to notice any more — well, they no longer say anything — and if they did, you and I are thicker skinned and very slightly numb.

Brenda Saunders

LANDSCAPE

The plane flies low over a curve of red ochre country. Landforms scatter. A waterhole stretches the horizon. Trees flash by in a line of grey. My window lifts to frame the sky, dips to saltpans turning blue after rain. The perspective tilts, pulls a mine into focus. Moving like ants, giant loaders dredge the inside out of the iron ore plain. Tailings bury a world of stillness, reshape a landscape of tussock grass, Spinifex rings holding the desert in place. At a slow angle man-made hills rise to meet us. Blow raw dust into a heaving sky.

Sarah St Vincent Welch

INSIDE

inside a fissure it tears across it's honest at least a bite

inside a scar the drill slipped here shadows jump wince

inside pink infection along the open edge flesh weeps

inside it is rank stinks festers delicious sticky threads

inside it's a psyche ripped it limps totters under here

inside it's a banshee silenced wailing in wound cuts

inside it's a torn mucous membrane unfit a fissure

inside it's an abscess empty a pit a crater a vent

inside it's a flap and under caress the tongue tip

inside it's a noise a grunt tic caught between

inside it's awkward as anything it's hard too

inside it's sticking out good you can't see it much

inside it's familiar even comforting sometimes

inside it's stemmed with soft cloth stitches tape

inside it's have a look ragged edged ulcers get a torch

inside it's life it's now a map of near misses closing over

Biographies

CAROLYN ABBS is a Western Australian poet. Her collection *The Tiny Museums* is published with UWA Publishing, 2017.

SHAYNAH ANDREWS was the winner of the 2018 Newcastle Short Story Award, and is currently completing her Creative Writing PhD at University of Newcastle. She is working on a collection of short stories set in Stockton, NSW.

DANIELLE BALDOCK's atmospheric writings capture small and vivid moments of time. She is published in Spineless Wonders' Landmarks and Shuffle anthologies, lives in Sydney and takes lots of photos. Her favourite colour is green.

MAGDALENA BALL is Managing Editor of Compulsive Reader. She is the author of several books of poetry and fiction, including, most recently *Hire Wire Step* (Flying Island Press) and *Unreliable Narratives* (Girls on Key Press).

STUART BARNES' first book Glasshouses (UQP) won the Thomas Shapcott Poetry Prize, was shortlisted for the Mary Gilmore Award and commended for the Anne Elder Award. He is currently working on a second poetry collection, *Form & Function*, and a novel. @StuartABarnes

JOHN BLACKHAWK is a canine behavioural therapist living in Umina Beach on the NSW Central Coast. His poetry collections include *Against The Currents* and *Dogs Barking In The Distance* (Ginninderra Press).

KATHLEEN BLEAKLEY lives between the escarpment and ocean, with celestial twin star 'pling. Her fifth collection of poetry/prose *letters* will be released November 2020.

JUDE BRIDGE has recently been published in the anthology, *The Colours of Katherine*. Being a hobbit, she is drawn to microlit as she finds big things overwhelming and self-important. jude-bridge.com

JULIE CHEVALIER writes arty poetry and flashy fiction in Sydney. She is the author of three collections and co-editor of three anthologies. Her passion is helping asylum seekers find jobs.

CHRIS CODY is an emerging writer of short stories currently undertaking his PhD in Creative Writing at Deakin University. He has short fiction published in various literary journals including *Southerly* and *The New Guard Literary Review*, and was a semi-finalist in the US-based Machigonne Fiction Contest in 2015. He lives in regional Victoria.

PAUL COLLIS is a Barkindji person, born in Bourke, NSW. He is currently a researcher and teacher at University Canberra. Paul's first novel, *Dancing Home*, won the 2017 David Unipon Award and was ACT Book of The Year in 2018.

SHADY COSGROVE is the author of *What the Ground Can't Hold* (Picador, 2013) and She Played Elvis (Allen and Unwin, 2009), which was shortlisted for the Australian Vogel Award. Her short fiction has appeared in *Best Australian Stories*, *Overland*, *Antipodes*, *Southerly* and other Spineless Wonders' anthologies.

JEN CRAIG has previously published micro-pieces, short stories, a novel, and a novella, *Panthers and the Museum of Fire* (Spineless Wonders, 2015), which was longlisted for the 2016 Stella Prize. She teaches English at TAFENSW.

TEREZA CRVENKOVIC has a background in philosophy, performance studies, yoga and dance. A recipient of two kidney transplants, Tereza aims to articulate stories from the lived experience of her body.

JUDITH NANGALA CRISPIN is a poet and visual artist, of Bpangerang descent, currently poetry editor of *The Canberra Times*. She lives is a farmhouse near Lake George with her family, two cats, a fat labrador and a dingo she rescued from the desert. Judith has two published collections of poems, *The Myrrh-Bearers* (Sydney: Puncher & Wattmann, 2015), and *The Lumen Seed* (New York: Daylight Books, 2017).

JAN DEAN's recent published work includes *FemAsia* and Not Very Quiet (online); *Eucalypt* a tanka journal issues 26 and 27, plus *Shuffle* (Spineless Wonders) as winner of the 2019 Hunter section.

DAN DISNEY teaches with the English Literature program at Sogang University, in Seoul.

JOSH (MEI-LING) DUBRAU researches and writes poetry around the areas of subjectivity, voice and lyric poetry. Her critical and creative work has appeared in *Overland*, *Southerly*, *Cordite*, *Computer Music Journal* and others. Josh writes e-poems for iPad apps, and has taught creative writing at the Universities of Wollongong and New South Wales.

GABRIELLE LORRAINE FLETCHER is a *Gundungurra* Traditional Custodian from the Blue Mountains of N.S.W and an Associate Professor (Indigenous Studies) at Deakin University. Academic and creative writer, eternally underpinned by the cultural responsibility of remembering.

ANNA FORSYTH is an editor and writer from New Zealand living in NSW. She is the founder of Girls on Key, a feminist poetry organisation and the editor for Girls on Key Press. Her poems and short stories have been published in *Landfall*, *Poetry NZ*, *FourW* and in print and online. Her latest poetry collection is *Beatific Toast.*

DOMINIQUE HECQ grew up in the French-speaking part of Belgium. She now lives in Melbourne. Her works include a novel, three collections of short stories and eight books of poetry. *After Cage* (2019) is her most recent collection. She is a recipient of the 2018 International Best Poets Prize, International Poetry Translation and Research Centre.

PAUL HETHERINGTON's most recent books are *Moonlight on Oleander: Prose Poems and Palace of Memory: An Elegy*. He is Professor of Writing at the University of Canberra and founded the International Prose Poetry Group in 2014.

SIOBHAN HODGE has a Ph.D. in English literature and was winner of the 2017 Kalang Eco-Poetry Award. She has had poetry published in a range of places, including *Overland*, *Westerly*, *Cordite* and *Southerly*.

RICHARD HOLT's micro-fiction collection, *What You Might Find* (Spineless Wonders, 2018) was described by The Australian's Ed Wright as 'a tonic for readers in search of new angles from which to spin the world around in their heads'. When not writing he creates text-based installations and performances in public spaces.

CHRISTINE HOWE is a writer and lecturer who teaches Creative Writing at the University of Wollongong. Her poetry and other short works have been published in journals such as *Cordite*; the *Griffith Review*; and *Law, Text, Culture*; and her first novel, *Song in the Dark*, was published by Penguin.

ANNA KERDIJK NICHOLSON's third book is *Everyday Epic* (Puncher & Wattmann). *Possession*, her second, received the 2010 Victorian Premier's Prize and Wesley Michel Wright Prize. She farms near Goulburn, NSW.

STEVE KINNANE has been an active researcher and writer for over 25 years. His interests are diverse encompassing history, creative documentary and sustainable livelihoods. Steve is a Marda Marda from Miriwoong country in the Kimberley.

BENJAMIN LAIRD is a software developer and poet. His poems and essays have been published in various print and online journals.

RAELEE LANCASTER is a writer, collaborator and creative producer based in Brisbane. Her work has been published in *The Guardian*, *The Saturday Paper*, *Overland*, *The Lifted Brow*, and more. Raised on Awabakal land, she is of Wiradjuri, Biripi and European descent.

ROSANNA LICARI is a writer and poet. Her work has appeared in various Australian and international journals including the Vice-Chancellor's International Poetry Prize 2019 Anthology, *e:ratio* (US), *Shearsman* (UK) and *Wild Court* (UK). She is the poetry editor of online literary journal *StylusLit*.

BRENDA MATTICK is a communications freelancer who 'loves words and pictures'. She is readjusting to life back in Australia after working for seven years in South East Asia under the Australian Volunteers for International Development program.

SUSAN MCCREERY has written three books: *Waiting for the Southerly* (poetry, Ginninderra, 2012), *Loopholes* (microfiction, Spineless Wonders, 2016) and *This Person Is Not That Person* (short stories, Puncher & Wattmann, 2019). She is working on her first novel.

MEGAN MCGRATH is an award-winning fiction writer from Minjerribah (North Stradbroke Island). She has written for *The New York Times*, *Meanjin*, and *Griffith Review*. Her short story collection, *All Hands*, is published by Spineless Wonders, 2019.

OLIVER MESTITZ makes music as The Finks. He lives and works on the stolen land of the Wurundjeri people of the Kulin Nation.

ALYSON MILLER teaches writing and literature at Deakin University, Melbourne. Her work has appeared in both national and international publications, alongside a recent collection of prose poems, titled *Strange Creatures* (Recent Work Press, 2019).

MARK O'FLYNN is a novelist and poet. His collection, *White Light* was published by Spineless Wonders in 2013. His latest collection of short stories *Dental Tourism*, published by Puncher & Wattmann.

TRISHA PENDER is an Associate Professor of English and Writing at the University of Newcastle. *Bibliophilic*, a chapbook, is published as part of Puncher & Wattman's Slow Loris series (2018), and two academic monographs, *Early Modern Women's Writing* and the *Rhetoric of Modesty* (2012) and *"I'm Buffy and You're History": Buffy the Vampire Slayer and Contemporary Feminism* (2016).

BRENDA PROUDFOOT is a Hunter writer, who has a desire to write experimental fiction. Her short stories and creative non-fiction have been published by Catchfire Press, the Newcastle Herald and the Hunter Writers Centre.

KA REES writes poetry and short fiction. Her work has been included by *Australian Poetry*, *Cordite Poetry Review*, Margaret River Press, *Overland*, *Review of Australian Fiction* and *Yalobusha Review*, among others. Kate lives in Sydney.

ANDREW ROFF's fiction has appeared in *Griffith Review*, *Overland*, *Southerly* and *Going Down Swinging* among others, and he was shortlisted for the Wakefield Press Unpublished Manuscript Award at the 2016 Adelaide Festival Awards for Literature.

COLLEEN RUSSELL is a Sydney based wordsmith writing in the fields of poetry, short stories and memoirs.

BRENDA SAUNDERS enjoys writing prose poems and micro fiction. Her poetry appears in major anthologies and journals such as *Australian Poetry, Westerly, Southerly* and *Overland*. She reviews for *Verity La*, *Mascara* and *Plumwood Mountain*.

NADINE SCHOFIELD is an emerging writer from Wollongong. She is helping young women find the magic of words and the power of their story. Nadine is completing a Master of Writing at Swinburne University.

AEDAN SIEBERT lives in South Australia and enjoys the sound of extremely heavy metal. He has previously worked for a rock and metal web-zine where he wrote album reviews and conducted interviews with interesting music personalities.

SARAH ST VINCENT WELCH is a Canberra-based writer, editor and image-maker. Her 'The Wedding Dress' was part of Spineless Wonders' 'Humans of Parramatta,' and was inspired by the wedding dress shops around Leichardt. Her chapbook *Open* was published by Rochford Press in 2019.

SAMUEL WAGAN WATSON is a Brisbane-based author of *Germanic and Indigenous heritage* who was the recipient of the 2018 Patrick White Literary Prize.

DEB WAIN is a writer who lives, and writes, on acreage on Taungurung country while being kept company by one human, five chooks, two dogs, many kangaroos and the occasional echidna. She teaches tertiary Creative Writing.

PATRICK WEST is a Melbourne based writer of short stories, poetry and prose poetry. His short-story collection, *The World Swimmers,* was praised by *The Australian* for its 'incredible insight into the human condition throughout'.

JESSICA L. WILKINSON is the author of three poetic biographies, *Marionette: A Biography of Miss Marion Davies, Suite for Percy Grainger* and *Music Made Visible: A Biography of George Balanchine*. She teaches Creative Writing at RMIT University.

Editor

CASSANDRA ATHERTON is an award-winning writer, academic and critic. She was a Harvard Visiting Scholar in English in 2016 and her most recent books of prose poetry are *Pika-Don* (Mountains Brown Press, 2017), *Prosody: Metre* (Recent Work Press, 2018) and *Pre-Raphaelite* (Garron Publishing, 2018).

She has judged many literary awards, including the Victorian Premier's Literary Awards: Prize for Poetry, The Lord Mayor's Prize for Poetry and the *Australian Book Review* Elizabeth Jolley short story competition.

The joanne burns Award

Each year Spineless Wonders auspices an award for the best writing in the forms of prose poem and microfiction in honour of foremost Australian experimental poet, joanne burns. The award is open to people residing in Australia and to Australians living overseas. Finalists chosen by each year's judging panel are offered publication in our annual anthology alongside invited writers.

The inaugural *joanne burns Award* was held in 2011 and was judged by joanne burns who selected Charles D'Anastasi's 'Madame Bovary' as the winning entry and commended Erin Gough's 'William Shatner vows to save the Great Basin Pocket Mouse' and Clare McHugh's 'Briefly'. All three pieces, along with those of other finalists appear in *small wonder*, edited by Linda Godfrey and Julie Chevalier.

The *2012 joanne burns Award* was judged by Carol Jenkins who selected Mark O'Flynn's 'under the maw of luna park' as the winning entry and commended Richard Holt's 'bush burial', Trina Denner's 'playing outside', Stu Hatton's 'down south' and Paul Mitchell's 'The Old Man and the Pool'. The winner and finalists all appear in *Stoned Crows & other Australian Icons*, edited by Julie Chevalier and Linda Godfrey.

The *2013 joanne burns Award* was judged by Shady Cosgrove who selected Mark Smith's '42 to Sydenham' as the winning entry and Hilary Hewitt's 'happy' and Mark Robert's 'cities that are not Dublin' as runners-up. All three pieces, along with those of other finalists appear in *Writing to the Edge*, edited by Linda Godfrey and Ali Jane Smith.

In *2014, The joanne burns Award* was judged by Angela Meyer and Richard Holt who selected Susan McCreery's 'Hold Up' as the winning entry and Kirsten Tranter's 'Turing Test Study Guide' and Mark Smith's 'The Meteorologist's Daughter' as runners up. All three pieces, along with those of other finalists are published in *Flashing the Square*, edited by Linda Godfrey and Bronwyn Mehan.

The 2015 joanne burns Award was judged by Kirsten Tranter who selected Nick Couldwell's 'Dancing' as the winning entry. Runners up were Tim Heffernan for 'Butterflies in Iraq' and Matthew Gabriel for 'jesussaves82'. All three pieces, along with those of other finalists and invited contributors are published in *Out of Place* edited by Kirsten Tranter and Linda Godfrey.

The 2016 joanne burns Microlit Award was co-sponsored by the Newcastle Writers Festival. The national category, judged by Cassandra Atherton, was won by Tim Heffernan for 'Barunga Conversation' and the Newcastle category, judged by Karen Whitelaw and Joanna Atherfold Finn, was won by Dael Allison for 'Breakwall'. The winning entries and finalists from both categories as well as invited contributors are published in *Landmarks* edited by Cassandra Atherton.

The 2017 joanne burns Microlit Award was co-sponsored by the Newcastle Writers Festival and judged by Cassandra Atherton. The national category was won by Tess Pearson for 'Traces' and the Hunter category was won by Luke Evans for 'You Can't Go

Back'. The winning entries and finalists from both categories as well as invited contributors are published in *Time* edited by Cassandra Atherton.

The 2018 joanne burns Microlit Award was co-sponsored by the Newcastle Writers Festival and judged by Cassandra Atherton. The national category was won by Brenda Saunders for 'Birding' and the Hunter category was won by Jan Dean for 'Fish Flops and Flaps'. The winning entries and finalists from both categories as well as invited contributors are published in *Shuffle* edited by Cassandra Atherton.

The 2019 joanne burns Microlit Award was co-sponsored by the Newcastle Writers Festival and judged by Cassandra Atherton. The national category was won by K A Rees for 'No White M & Ms' and the Hunter category was won by Shaynah Andrews for 'The Ocean Has Made Promises'. The winning entries and finalists from both categories as well as invited contributors are published in *Scars* edited by Cassandra Atherton.

About joanne burns

joanne burns grew up in Sydney's eastern suburbs. She worked as an English teacher in New South Wales, and for a time in London. She has taught creative writing in tertiary institutions, schools and community organisations. Her first collection of poems, *Snatch*, was published in London in 1972 Since then she has published more than a dozen further books of poetry. Her poems have appeared in numerous Australian literary journals, poetry magazines and have been set for study on the Higher School Certificate syllabus. joanne has been particularly concerned with the blurring of the distinctions between poetry and prose in her work, and has written extensively in prose poem/ microfiction forms. She has also written monologues and short futurist fictions and 'farables' (fables/ parables). Her latest collection *Brush* was published by Giramondo Poets in 2014. In 2016, she was awarded the New South Wales Premier's Kenneth Slessor Literary Award for Poetry. The latest collection of her work *apparently* was published by Giramondo Poetry in 2019.

Acknowledgements

We wish congratulate all finalists in the 2019 Newcastle Writers Festival/joanne burns Microlit Award and to thank all of the writers who entered the competition and who continue to support the microlit form and publishing house, Spineless Wonders.

Thank you to Rosemarie Milsom, director of the Newcastle Writers Festival and her team for her foresight in sponsoring this award and her phenomenal work in bringing it to the fabu¬lous Newcastle Writers Festival – one of the finest and most supportive writers' festivals in Australia.

Thank you to the commissioned writers: Julie Chevalier, Paul Collis, Shady Cosgrove, Judith Nangala Crispin, Dan Disney, Gabrielle Fletcher, Paul Hetherington, Siobhan Hodge, Richard Holt, Steve Kinnane, Benjamin Laird, Raelee Lancaster, Alyson Miller, Brenda Saunders, Samuel Wagan Watson, Deb Wain, Patrick West and Jessica Wilkinson.

Thank you to Bettina Kaiser for her evocative cover design. And special thanks to our production assistant, Linda Bathish.

As ever, thank you to joanne burns, after whom this award is named. joanne is a pioneer and ambassador of the short form and her luminous, witty and innovative microlit is enduring.

Bronwyn Mehan (Publisher) and Cassandra Atherton (Editor), 2020

This project has been assisted by the Australian Government through the Australia Council, its arts funding and advisory body.

Find more microlit at
SPINELESS WONDERS
www.shortaustralianstories.com.au

Spineless Wonders publications are available in print and digital format from participating bookshops and online. For further information, go to the Spineless Wonders website:

www.shortaustralianstories.com.au